Old Jack's Ghost Stories from England (1)

I Talk You Talk Press

CONTENTS

ACKNOWLEDGMENTS

With sincere thanks to Colin Dixon who collected and recorded the stories contained in this volume. Without his contribution this book would not have been possible.

WHO IS OLD JACK?

Old Jack lives in the north of England. He is an old man now. He likes strange stories. He spends his days reading his books and visiting old places around the UK and Ireland. He likes to go to places where he can hear mysterious stories. He also likes to go to places with ghosts.

When Old Jack goes out, he sits quietly on buses, trains and in cafes. He listens to people talking. Sometimes, he hears some very interesting and unusual stories.

If you go to an old town in the north of England, and you see an old man, sitting very quietly and thinking very deeply, remember, this might be Old Jack. He will listen very carefully to your stories. But you won't know that he is listening. You will just think he is an old man sitting alone at the next table in the café or the pub. When he goes home, he will write the stories he has heard in his special ghost story book.

This book has six of Old Jack's ghost stories from England. Old Jack will tell you the six stories in his own words. He hopes you enjoy his mysterious stories, and he hopes that, if you visit England, you will go to some of the places in the stories, and return home with some interesting stories to tell your family and friends.

1. THE PLUMBER'S STORY

Place: Treasurer's House, York, North Yorkshire

I'm Old Jack. My book of ghost stories starts in a very old city.

The Romans came here in AD71. That's nearly 2000 years ago. They called the city *Eboracum*. Later, the Vikings came. They called the city *Jorvik*, and today, we call it *York*.

York is a very historic city in North Yorkshire in the north of England. It has a cathedral (large church), called York Minster, and many old narrow streets. These streets have not changed for 1000 years. If you go to York today, you will see many tourists from around the world. They walk along the streets, take photographs and stop for a cup of tea in one of the small tea shops. It is a very popular tourist spot.

Of course, if you go to York, I recommend you visit York Minster, walk along the old Roman city walls and enjoy tea and shopping in the old streets. York is a very good place to buy presents for your family and friends. You will also get some wonderful photographs.

But there is another place I recommend. That place is behind York Minster, away from the busy tourist area. Walk down the quiet street behind the cathedral, and you will see the Treasurer's House.

In this house, you can see many old antiques and pieces of furniture. These items belonged to a private owner who lived here around a hundred years ago. However, long before this time, until 1547, the house contained expensive and important religious items and treasures from York Minster.

The Treasurer's House has a history of 2000 years. It also has a ghost story. I think this is one of England's strangest and most interesting ghost stories.

Let's go back to 1953. The Treasurer's House is old, and needs some repairs. In the cellar, the room under the house, a young plumber is checking the water pipes. The floor of the cellar is not smooth, so he must be very careful. One part of the cellar floor is low. The other part of the floor is high.

The lights are on, and he is working very hard. He hears a sound. *What was that?* he thinks. It sounds like a horn, or a trumpet. *Maybe it is a car on the road outside,* he thinks. He continues to work. Then, he hears the sound again. This time, the sound is louder.

He looks around the cellar. The sound of the horn, or trumpet, is growing much louder. The lights are on, so he can see very well. He sees something move near the back wall.

"What is that?" he says to himself.

Suddenly, a man comes out of the wall! He is wearing a helmet and the clothes of a Roman soldier. The young plumber is very frightened. He falls off his ladder. Then, another soldier comes out of the wall. He is riding a horse. And behind him, there are around twenty more soldiers. They are walking slowly and silently. The young plumber cannot see their feet. They look like they are walking on their knees. Then, they walk to the lower part of the floor. Now, the plumber can see their feet. The soldiers are wearing sandals with laces. The laces go up to their knees. He looks at their weapons. They are carrying spears and large round shields. He looks at their faces. They look tired, dirty, and very sad.

The soldiers disappear into the opposite wall. When the last soldier disappears, the frightened young plumber runs upstairs.

The manager of the building looks at his frightened face.

"You have just seen our Roman ghosts, haven't you?" he says to the plumber. "Other people have seen the Roman ghosts too."

The young plumber's story became famous. Roman history experts had different ideas about the story and the soldiers. Some experts believed the plumber's story. They said, "An old Roman road goes through the cellar on the lower part of the floor. The plumber saw the soldiers on this old road."

Other experts did not believe the plumber's story. They said, "It is not true. Roman soldiers in that area of England did not have sandals with laces to their knees. They had sandals with laces to their ankles.

They did not carry round shields. They had rectangular shields."

So, for a long time, not many people believed the young plumber. However, years later, Roman experts found some items near a place called Hadrian's Wall, which is north of York. The items were from Roman soldiers from different areas of the Roman Empire. These Roman soldiers from different areas walked north to Hadrian's Wall. When they were going to the wall, they stayed at Eboracum, and they walked on the old Roman road. And, these Roman soldiers from different areas had sandals with laces up to their knees, and round shields.

Did the young plumber see these tired soldiers walking along the old Roman road? I think he did. The soldiers were cold and tired. Maybe they died on the old Roman road. Maybe they died before they arrived at Hadrian's Wall. And so, even today, they continue to try to walk to Hadrian's Wall along the old road in the cellar...

So, if you ever visit the Treasurer's House, and you hear the sound of a trumpet, remember this story...

2. THE HEADLESS WOMAN

Place: Duddon, Cheshire, England

Let's travel to the county of Cheshire in North West England now. The famous city of Chester is in Cheshire. Like York, Chester is a Roman city and many tourists from all over the world visit it. Chester also has many ghost stories. I will tell you one of Chester's most frightening ghost stories in *Old Jack's Ghost Stories from England (2)*.

But today, I want to tell you a story from a quiet country village called Duddon. This village is about five miles from Chester.

The road from Chester to Duddon takes you into the countryside, through fields and farmland. Today, the road from Chester to Duddon is very busy. But, let's try to imagine the village nearly 400 years ago at the time of the English Civil War.

In this war, King Charles I (the first) was fighting Oliver Cromwell and the army of the government. This army travelled around the country trying to kill people who supported the king.

Near Duddon, there was a large country house called Hockenhull Hall. The family who lived in this grand hall was very rich, and the family members were supporters of the king.

They had a very nice life. They lived in a large house and had lots of money and servants. But one day, their lives changed forever. They heard some very bad news: "Oliver Cromwell's army is coming!"

"What shall we do? Should we stay? Should we go?" they asked each other.

"It's too dangerous! We should go!" said someone.

5

"But what about our silver? What about our treasure? If we leave it here, the army will take it!" said another person.

They thought about what to do. Then, someone had an idea.

"Let's put the treasure and silver in a secret place! We can tell one of the servants about the secret place. Then, when the army has gone, we can come back. And, we can keep our treasure!"

"Which servant shall we tell? Who can we trust?" asked someone.

Everyone thought for a few minutes. Then, someone said, "Grace! Grace Trigg! We can trust her! And she is a woman. The soldiers in the army won't hurt a woman. They will be nice to her!"

So, the family put the treasure and silver in a secret place. They told their trusted servant Grace about the secret place. Then, they left their home.

Very soon after, the soldiers came to Hockenhull Hall. They knew the family was very rich, so they searched for treasure. They looked everywhere, but they could not find anything. They became angrier and angrier.

"Where is the silver? Where is the family's treasure?" they asked Grace. "Where is it? Tell us!"

But Grace was a loyal servant. She would not tell the soldiers.

So, the soldiers took Grace away from the hall and they attacked her. They beat her for two days. But still Grace would not say anything. Some soldiers became very angry, and one day, near an inn, one of them took a sword, and cut off Grace's head.

Ever since that terrible day, the ghost of Grace has been seen walking in the dark fields between Hockenhull Hall and the inn.

This inn in Duddon became a pub and a restaurant. It was called "The Headless Woman." When I was younger, I enjoyed drinking beer there and listening to the stories of the local people. Unfortunately, the pub closed a few years ago.

Many people have seen the ghost of Grace. They say that she carries her head under her arm as she walks the lonely path from the hall to the inn.

Why does she appear? Maybe she is looking for the family of the house. Maybe she wants to tell the family that she did not tell the army about the treasure and silver.

But whatever the reason, many car drivers have seen her, as they drive along the busy road. They often slow down, unsure of what they are seeing, and when they try to look more closely, the ghostly figure of Grace slowly fades...

If you visit Chester, go for a drive to Duddon. But, if you go at night, be very careful. Some drivers suddenly see a woman in front of their cars. They stop because they think, "Oh no! I hit someone!" They get out of their cars, but there is no one there...

3. THE SAD LOVERS

Place: The Prince Rupert Hotel, Shrewsbury, Shropshire

Let's leave North West England, and travel to the Midlands. We are going to Shrewsbury, a historic market town in the county of Shropshire.

This charming town has many old and narrow passages which connect the busy streets. Shrewsbury is a famous town in England. Charles Darwin was born here. The town is also famous for its many ghost stories.

In a street called Butcher's Row, there is a famous hotel called The Prince Rupert Hotel. In the 17th century, this hotel was an inn. During the English Civil War, Prince Rupert, the nephew of King Charles I (the first), came from Germany to help his uncle, and he stayed here.

The hotel is very old. Some parts of the hotel date from the 12th century. Others date from the 15th century.

The Prince Rupert Hotel has many ghosts. I will tell you about two of the ghosts. These ghosts have very sad stories.

One ghost is in Room 7. It is the ghost of a young man. Many years ago, the young man was staying at the hotel. He had a girlfriend, whom he loved very much. He was very happy because they were going to get married.

The night before his wedding, he was staying at the hotel. He was looking forward to his wedding day and he was very excited. But that night, before he went to sleep, he heard some terrible news. His girlfriend was in love with his best friend. She decided to cancel the

8

wedding. She left the young man, and disappeared with his friend. The young man was very upset. After hearing the news, he decided that he didn't want to live anymore. He didn't want to live without the woman he loved. So, that night, when the town was silent, and the other guests were asleep, all alone in his hotel room, this young man killed himself.

Today, some hotel guests say that strange things happen in Room 7. Some guests say they have seen the young man, and felt his sadness fill the room...

But he is not the only ghost in the hotel with a sad story about love.

One of the hotel's most famous ghosts is in Room 6. Long ago, a young servant girl lived in Room 6. She was engaged to a young man. She was looking forward to their wedding day and to a life with the man she loved. But just before the wedding, the young man left her. He decided that he didn't want to marry her. The girl was very upset. She sat in her room and cried and cried. Other servants in the house were very worried about her. They knocked on her door, but she didn't answer. So, they opened the door. They all screamed very loudly. The girl was hanging from the ceiling. She had killed herself.

This happened a long time ago, but some people say that the girl has not disappeared...

Imagine you are staying in Room 6 of the Prince Rupert Hotel. One night, you wake up and see shoes, a long skirt, and the body of a woman, turning around on a rope just above your head...

What would you do? I think I would run to the bar and have a few glasses of whisky.

4. THE ATTIC

Place: Ettington Park Hotel, near Stratford-upon-Avon, Warwickshire

As we travel around England, let's stop in Warwickshire in the Midlands. This county has beautiful scenery and is full of history and stories. It is also one of England's main tourist places. Why? Well, in Warwickshire is Stratford-upon-Avon, the home of one of the most famous Englishmen, William Shakespeare.

Three million people visit Stratford-upon-Avon every year. They enjoy watching plays at the Royal Shakespeare Theatre, visiting Shakespeare's house, and walking around the museum in the home of Anne Hathaway, Shakespeare's wife.

Where would you like to stay if you visited Stratford-upon-Avon? Would you like to stay in a hotel in the town? Or would you like to travel a few miles through the English countryside and stay in a grand old building? In a building with many strange stories, and some old residents...residents who are hundreds of years old?

Our story is from the Ettington Park Hotel. This building is a few miles from Stratford-upon-Avon. It was built in the 12th century. In its long history, it has been a family home, an old people's home, a prisoner of war camp during the Second World War, a nightclub and hotel. Maybe you have seen this building. In 1963, it appeared in a famous horror movie called *The Haunting.*

In 1979, a fire destroyed the building, but very soon after, in 1983, it opened again. This time, it became a luxury hotel.

The shadows of time are long at the Ettington Park Hotel, and there have been many strange events.

Some people have heard women's voices in another room. When they go into the room, there is no one there. Other people have seen books flying in the library! Some people also say that the temperature suddenly falls, and they feel very cold. A few people have seen the ghost of Mary, a servant girl from many years ago, who fell down the stairs and died.

In a corridor, some people have seen the ghosts of two children who drowned in the nearby river in 1800. Other people have seen and heard these children in other areas of the hotel.

A few years ago, I was sitting in a pub in Stratford-upon-Avon. I was alone. At the next table there were two men. They were drinking and talking about the Ettington Park Hotel. I listened carefully. One of the men had an interesting story.

He said, "I was staying in a very old room at the Ettington Park Hotel. I couldn't sleep because the guests in the room above were very noisy. They were walking about, shutting doors loudly and screaming.

"I was very angry, and went downstairs to complain to the night manager. I told the manager my room name and number.

"The manager looked at me for a few seconds. Then, he said, 'But Sir, there is no room above yours. There is only an old, empty attic.' Later, I heard a story. 200 years ago, a woman was hanged in the attic above my room..."

The man finished talking. His friend was silent.

I finished my beer and left the pub. It was about 11 o' clock at night, and the autumn wind was cold. As I walked through the dark and quiet streets of Stratford-upon-Avon, I thought, *Who was the woman? Maybe the man in the pub heard the woman from 200 years ago. Maybe she comes back at night, to the place where she died...*

On the way back to my hotel, I walked past Shakespeare's house.

I thought, *Yes, Shakespeare had some good stories. But there are many more stories in this town. Many more strange stories...*

5. THE UNSEEN MAN

Place: Liverpool Street Station, The London Underground, London

Now let's travel south, to London. This city is very famous for its beautiful historic sightseeing spots, such as Buckingham Palace, the Tower of London, Westminster, and Big Ben. You can hear the echoes of the past when you walk around its streets.

For this story, we leave the historic buildings and busy shopping streets, and go down under the city. People say that here, in the dark tunnels under the city, there are many ghosts and spirits.

In New York, it is called the Subway. In Paris, it is called the Metro. And to the people of London who use it every day, it is called the Underground.

The London Underground railway system was the world's first underground railway. It was built in 1863. Since then, there have been many accidents and very bad events in the long, dark tunnels under the streets of London. Building the Underground was a very dangerous job. Many workers died there. There have also been train accidents, fires, murders and suicides.

And there is more darkness lying under the streets of London. From 1665-66, there was a terrible disease in London. It was called the Great Plague. This disease killed over 100,000 people. Many of these people were buried under the streets of London. They were buried together in "pits".

Two hundred years later, when workers were building the tunnels, they found many of these pits, with bodies of the people who died of the plague. Some say that the tunnels of the Underground are next to the pits, and that there are many more...

So, there are many stories of ghosts and spirits of people who died in the Underground, or were buried under the city after the terrible disease. People say that some of these people return today, to walk along the dark tunnels.

Let's go back to a hot summer night in the year 2000.

It is 2:00am, and the station has closed. All the trains have stopped running. A night employee is watching the security camera screens. We don't know his name, but let's call him George. He looks at the screen of the camera on the platform. There is a man on the platform. He is standing very still. It looks like he is waiting for a train. George is very shocked. He picks up the telephone and calls another night employee. We will call him Andrew.

George says, "There is a man standing on the platform. Please take him out of the station. Tell him that the station is closed."

"OK, I will go there now," says Andrew. He goes to the platform, but the platform is empty. He cannot see the man. He checks all the gates and doors. They are locked. He calls George from a telephone on the platform.

"There is no one here," he says.

In the security room, George is still watching the screens. "But there is a man! He is standing next to you! I can see him on the screen!" he says.

Andrew looks around the platform again. He cannot see anyone. He searches the platform again. He doesn't find anything. He calls George.

"There is no one here," he says.

George watches Andrew walk past the man. Then, the man starts to fade and disappear.

George and Andrew cannot explain the strange events of that night in 2000. And they cannot explain the white clothes which suddenly appeared on a bench on the platform when Andrew went back to the platform to check for a third time...

When I visit London, I leave the busy streets and go down to the Underground. I am old now, so I can't walk very far. The Underground is a fast and convenient way for me to travel around the city. As the train travels from station to station, I think about London's dark secrets. Who are these ghosts and spirits that stay down here? What happened to them when they were alive? And why can't they escape the dark tunnels of this busy and modern city?

6. THE BLUE LADY

Place: Macdonald Berystede Hotel, Ascot, Berkshire

For our last story, we leave the city of London, and go west to the village of Ascot. This village is very famous for the Royal Ascot horse race. The race has been held every year since 1711. It is very near to Windsor Castle, and has connections with the royal family. The Queen and other members of the royal family attend this race every year.

Near the famous racecourse, there is an elegant hotel called Macdonald Berystede Hotel. Long ago, it was the home of a very rich family. Now, people say it is one of the most beautiful hotels in Berkshire. They also say it is the most haunted...

The year was 1886. Very early one morning, when everyone was asleep, there was a fire. Everyone woke up and escaped from the building. They stood outside, watching the terrible fire spread through the grand old house.

The lady of the house had a maid. The maid was a woman called Eliza Kleininger.

When she was watching the fire, she remembered something...the jewellery.

I must get my jewellery from the house! she thought. *I can't let my jewellery be destroyed!*

Eliza ran into the burning house to get her jewellery box. People shouted to her, "Come back! Don't go into the house!" But Eliza did not listen to them.

The jewellery was very important to Eliza. So important, that she went back into the house for it. Maybe it was her grandmother's jewellery. Or maybe it was a present from a rich person. Maybe Eliza was saving it for her future. We don't know, because Eliza never returned from the house. After the fire, servants found her dead body on the stairs. She was holding a jewellery box.

For many years, the house was a ruin. It was destroyed very badly in the fire. No one could live there. But local people started to see strange things around the old house. Some people saw a ghostly figure, wearing a blue dress, walking around the grounds near the building.

In 1903, the house was rebuilt. It became the Berystede Hotel. And that is when people started to talk about the "Blue Lady".

Guests at the hotel started to complain. They said that at around 3:00am, they could hear the sound of someone breathing heavily in the halls.

Who did they hear? Maybe they heard another guest running around. But I don't think so. I think the guests heard Eliza breathing as she rushed back into the house to get the jewellery…

Staff and some guests at the hotel have also seen a strange figure on the stairs. It is the figure of a Blue Lady. She is walking down the stairs, but she disappears before she reaches the bottom.

Who is this strange lady dressed in blue? I think it is the ghost of Eliza. Maybe she cannot leave the house without her jewellery. Every night, she tries to get her jewellery, but she cannot. Or maybe, she got the jewellery and she is trying to find the exit. But she cannot escape because the fire is so bad. She cannot breathe and she falls and dies, holding her precious jewellery. And so, her ghost stays forever, in the Berystede Hotel.

So, if you visit Windsor Castle, like many tourists do every year, why not take a trip to Ascot? You can see one of the world's most famous horse races. You might see the Queen. And you might see Eliza…

THANK YOU

Thank you for reading Old Jack's Ghost Stories from England (1).
(Word count: 4,324) Old Jack hopes you enjoyed reading his stories.

For more information about the places in this book, please visit
http://www.italk-youtalk.com. There is a page with maps and
photographs of the places that Old Jack has written about.

If you would like to read more graded readers, please visit our
website http://www.italkyoutalk.com

Other graded readers by Old Jack:
Old Jack's Ghost Stories from England (2)
Old Jack's Ghost Stories from Scotland
Old Jack's Ghost Stories from Wales
Old Jack's Ghost Stories from Ireland
Old Jack's Ghost Stories from Japan

NOTES AND REFERENCES

1. The Plumber's Tale.
The Treasurer's House, Minster Yard, York, YO1 7JL
The Treasurer's House is owned by the National Trust.
The story is based on information found on the following sites:
http://www.britannia.com/history/legend/yorkghosts/yorkgt05.html
(Retrieved May 2013)
http://www.visityork.org/York-Treasurer's-House/details/?dms=13&venue=1500176
(Retrieved May 2013)
http://www.nationaltrust.org.uk/treasurers-house-york/
(Retrieved May 2013)
http://www.real-british-ghosts.com/roman-ghosts.html
(Retrieved May 2013)

2. The Headless Woman
Tarporley Road, Duddon, Cheshire
The story is based on information found on the following site and in the following book:
http://www.chesterchronicle.co.uk/chester-news/local-chester-news/2009/02/27/paranormal-research-uk-investigators-look-for-ghosts-at-the-headless-woman-pub-in-duddon-59067-23020349/
(Retrieved May 2013)
Haughton, Brian. Famous Ghost Stories: Legends and Lore (New York: 2012, The Rosen Publishing Group Inc.) pg 58-59

3. The Sad Lovers

The Prince Rupert Hotel, Butcher Row, Shrewsbury, Shropshire, SY1 1UQ

The story is based on information found on the following sites and in the following book:

http://www.prince-rupert-hotel.co.uk/

(Retrieved May 2013)

http://www.shropshirestar.com/news/2009/01/13/hunting-ghosts-in-shrewsbury/ (Retrieved May 2013)

http://www.telegraph.co.uk/expat/expatpicturegalleries/8085718/Britains-most-haunted-hotels.html?image=5

(Retrieved May 2013)

http://www.guardian.co.uk/travel/2008/oct/14/haunted-hotels-uk

(Retrieved May 2013)

Nicolle, Dorothy. Shropshire Walks with Ghosts and Legends (Cheshire: 2003, Sigma Lesiure) pg 50-51

4. The Attic

Ettington Park Hotel, Alderminster, Stratford-upon-Avon, Warwickshire, CV37 8BU

The story is based on information found on the following sites:

http://www.handpickedhotels.co.uk/hotels/ettington-park-hotel/History/

(Retrieved May 2013)

http://www.telegraph.co.uk/expat/expatpicturegalleries/8085718/Britains-most-haunted-hotels.html?image=3

(Retrieved May 2013)

The story about the guest in the room below the attic is based on the story by "Stanley Smith", shown on the following sites:

http://www.birminghammail.co.uk/news/local-news/is-a-stratford-upon-avon-hotel-britains-most-haunted-225355

(Retrieved May 2013)

http://www.bbc.co.uk/coventry/content/articles/2006/06/29/weird_ettington_park_feature.shtml

(Retrieved May 2013)

5. The Unseen Man

Liverpool Street Underground Station, Central London Underground Ltd., Liverpool Street, London, EC2M 7PP

The story about the two workers is based on a story shown on the following sites:

http://www.unexplained-mysteries.com/column.php?id=135129 (Original story on this site © Mike Herffernan)

(Retrieved May 2013)

http://www.londonparanormal.com/underground

(Retrieved May 2013)

http://www.ukseries.com/blog/2012/12/regular-ghosts-on-the-london-underground/

(Retrieved May 2013)

The names of the workers, "George" and "Andrew" were created by us to simplify the retelling of the story.

6. The Blue Lady

Macdonald Berystede Hotel & Spa, Bagshot Road, Sunninghill, Ascot, Berkshire, SL5 9JH

http://www.macdonaldhotels.co.uk/our-hotels/macdonald-berystede-hotel-spa/

(Retrieved May 2013)

The story is based on information found on the following sites:

http://www.windsor.gov.uk/accommodation/macdonald-berystede-hotel-and-spa-p2243

(Retrieved May 2013)

http://www.questforghosts.com/haunted-houses/britain/the-berystede-hotel.html

(Retrieved May 2013)

http://www.information-britain.co.uk/haunteddetail.php?id=113

(Retrieved May 2013)

ABOUT THE AUTHOR

I Talk You Talk Press is a Japan-based publisher of language textbooks, graded readers and language learning/teaching resources.

Our team is made up of highly experienced language teachers and translators, who have all studied at least one additional language to an advanced level.

This experience enables us to design our materials from the perspective of both the teacher and the learner. We consult with both teachers and language learners when designing our textbooks and graded readers, and test our materials extensively in the classroom before publication.

We are a fast-growing press, and currently publish graded readers for learners of English. We publish new graded readers monthly.

www.ingramcontent.com/pod-product-compliance
Lightning Source LLC
Chambersburg PA
CBHW022352040426
42449CB00006B/846